The Little Book of

WORDPRESS SEO

+ Complete WordPress Setup Guide

+ Complete List of Tested Plug-ins

+ Complete, Working Configuration

+ SEO Guide for Blog Content

+ Social Media Optimization Guide

based on a popular WordPress blog

Kalin Nacheff

The Little Book of WordPress SEO

Copyright © 2012 by Kalin Nacheff

Printed in the United States of America

ISBN 978-1480217584

Designed and Illustrated by Kalin Nacheff

For more information and technical support, please contact the author:

kalin_nacheff@yahoo.com

ABOUT THE AUTHOR

Kalin Nacheff is a full-time professional blogger, WordPress developer, and writer. He is the creator and author of the Motorcycle Blog of Leatherup.com (http://blog.leatherup.com)—a popular blog about motorcycling and motorcycle culture. His other books include *How I Got Rid of Migraine Headaches in 30 Days*, a book about migraine management. He lives with his wife, Snezhana Nacheff, in Pasadena, California.

CONTENTS

INTRODUCTION

PART 1: INITIAL SETUP

CHAPTER 1: PERFORMANCE SETTINGS............7

PART 2: CONTENT SEO & MAINTENANCE

CHAPTER 3: CONTENT SEO...............................36

INTRODUCTION

General Description of This Book

This book offers a solution to a main problem with WordPress—how to optimize an existing or setup a new WordPress site for the search engines, social media, and your users—a complete step by step solution you can use on your current blog or site or on a brand new WordPress installation. The book offers a complete configuration (no complicated choices or trade-offs) that is tested and works smoothly, modeled after my successful motorcycle blog (Motorcycle Blog of Leatherup.com at http://blog.leatherup.com). I'm also offering advice for creating SEO optimized but user-centered content as well as advice on maintaining your Wordpress website. The focus is using plug-ins instead of the help of programmers to improve your site or solve problems and the book includes a complete list of tested plug-ins created by reputable developers with a short guide about using each plug-in. Some of these plug-ins help search engines find, crawl, and better index your site; some increase your site's speed, and others increase your site's security.

A website must be solid, useful, and beautiful is a statement I derive from the basic principles of architecture first described by Roman writer and architect Marcus Vitruvius, who said that a structure must have these three basic qualities. Every step I recommend throughout this book is aimed at achieving one of these qualities, and the collection of all steps tries to achieve an equilibrium, a good balance among them. Here's the connection between the basic Vitruvian qualities and the ones I often mention in the book: solidness (security), usefulness (good user experience, speed) and beauty (good user experience). Further connection can be made between specific, technical steps and the Vitruvian principles. For example, installing a plug-in that helps search engines crawl your WordPress website is aiming toward solidness (few people will see your site if it's not indexed by search engines).

How it Started

The interface of WordPress can be intuitively learned and used by most internet savvy people, but SEO (search engine optimization) can't. Think of the millions of WordPress blogs that have great content but are under-optimized because their authors and owners have little knowledge of SEO. This book can help anyone who is good at creating content with WordPress but lacks SEO knowledge.

I have blogged for years unaware of any of the techniques I talk about in this book. When I moved to the marketing department of my company Leatherup.com, I met Tim and Carl, two professionals each with their own special knowledge about search engine optimization. I had started a blog for our company (http://blog.leatherup.com) and little by little I began optimizing it, using advice from Tim and Carl. Because I wanted to use the same techniques for my personal blogs and for other projects, I started taking notes, a checklist of things I had to do right after

I install WordPress on a domain. And this was the material for the first two chapters and the last chapter (*Chapter 1 Performance Settings, Chapter 2 Security Settings,* and *Chapter 4 Maintenance & Further Development*). *Chapter 3 Content SEO* was modeled after a guide for maintaining a company blog that I created for my consulting business and used in a number of projects.

The Chapters

I divided the book into several chapters and two parts. *Chapter 1 Performance Settings* and *Chapter 2 Security Settings* focus on setting up your newly created WordPress site—a list of things you need to do before you start creating content. But I treat them separately because site security is different than site performance. In *Chapter 3 Content SEO,* I describe my posting routine, how I craft individual posts on WordPress. *Chapter 4 Maintenance & Further Development* shows things you have to perform regularly to keep your site clean and up to date, and things you can do to develop it further. I tried to stick to what this book is about—WordPress SEO and optimization, but I didn't want to leave out other ways of optimizing, especially off-site techniques, that would help any website. That's why I included *Appendix A*. In *Appendix B,* I'll show you how I set up banner ads for my WordPress blogs.

Using This Book as a Quick-Reference Checklist

I designed the book to look like a checklist of things you need to do in order of importance. I wanted it to be as simple and as useful to you as it was to me. Most of the items listed in the book are from my personal WordPresss Setup/SEO checklist. I didn't use any images in the book and kept it short and simple because I believe that the list form will be most useful to my audience.

About WordPress Plug-ins

WordPress plug-ins can help you optimize your site with little hassle and without the help of a programmer. But too many plug-ins will make your site less secure and slow. Plus, the more plug-ins you add, the harder it will be to find the cause of a problem and the more likely it will be that something will go wrong. The plug-ins I recommend work together well in harmony. I also mention other plug-ins that work well with other configurations but not mine and that I would definitely use if they worked with this configuration.

WordPress Blog vs. WordPress Website

Most of the time in this book, I talk about using WordPress to build and optimize a blog. Throughout the book, I use the words *WordPress blog* and *WordPress website* to mean the same thing.

On-Site vs. Off-Site SEO

Search engine optimization is traditionally divided into two main areas: on-site and off-site SEO. The former refers to SEO techniques you control on your website and the latter to SEO techniques you employ on external websites in order to rank your own. The terms on-page and off-page are also used, sometimes to mean exactly the same, and sometimes the word on-page can refer to the optimization of specific pages as opposed to the term on-site that can mean optimizing your site in general.

Although I did not provide chapters or explanations in other parts of this book dedicated to these two terms, this book contains advice on both on- and off-site SEO. For example, all the settings in *Chapter 1 Performance Settings* are on-site SEO, and the advice on sharing your WordPress blog posts on social media sites in *Chapter 3 Maintenance* can be classified as off-site SEO. *Appendix A* lists only off-site techniques.

Most of the techniques I describe throughout the book are on-site (or on-page) SEO.

Social Media's Optimization

This book also describes social media optimization (SMO) techniques, interwoven with SEO techniques. Check *Create Fully Optimized Posts and Pages, Chapter 3 Content SEO*. These days SMO is becoming more and more important because of the rapid growth of social sites like Facebook and Twitter. Social media brought a shift in focus for online presence and is now influencing search engines which are increasingly using what people like or dislike on social media in their own search algorithms. The best thing about social media is that if you have great content on your site, sooner or later this content will be discovered and shared by users. Just don't wait for social media users to find and share your site—you, as the author of the content, should be the first to share.

Black Hat vs. White Hat SEO

SEO techniques are sometimes classified as black hat (unethical and illegitimate) and white hat (ethical and allowed by search engines). Throughout this book, I only discuss SEO techniques that are ethical and allowed by search engines—all ways to legitimately improve and promote your WordPress website. The same applies to my techniques aimed at promoting your website via social media.

PART I

INITIAL SETUP

Part I of this book deals with settings and SEO techniques you should apply on a new WordPress installation.

CHAPTER 1

PERFORMANCE SETTINGS

1. Choose a WordPress Theme

The first thing on your to-do list after you install WordPress on a web hosting server should be replacing the default WordPress theme with a better one. WordPress themes are much more that design—in fact today they behave more or less like WordPress plug-ins. Just as plug-ins, themes have to be updated to function properly and to be secure against intrusion and hackers. Themes can solve many problems that would otherwise require the installation of plug-ins or the touch of a programmer. And when a theme does the job of several plug-ins, you get a number of benefits: it makes your website lighter, faster, and secure (with every new plug-in, your WordPress website becomes code-heavy, SEO-unfriendly, and more prone to cyber attacks). Good themes allow you to adjust the layout of your site and update the graphics and can serve as a platform for highly customized designs. Such themes are often referred to as WordPress theme frameworks. I recommend using an established premium theme framework—sold, updated, and supported by a reputable Word-Press developer company (Genesis by StudioPress or PageLines by PageLines).

Remember that a WordPress theme framework will allow you to update the design and look of your website whenever and how-ever you want, and you can use the help of professional graphic designers or programmers or both. But the best part is that the core files of your theme will be available for update (like a regu-lar plug-in) every time the developers come up with a new, im-proved, and more secure version.

In my motorcycle blog (http://blog.leatherup.com), I use a paid, professional version of PageLines theme framework. Well, in more technical terms, I use a child theme (http://codex.word-press.org/Child_Themes) of PageLines theme framework. I like PageLines because it allows me to build and customize a profes-sional WordPress website using a simple drag-and-drop tool. I don't need the help of a programmer to change the code, and because I'm skilled in creating graphics with Photoshop and Adobe Illustrator, I don't need a graphic designer too. I'm in full control of my theme. PageLine cost me $97 for a Professional/Personal License and a one-month free Plus Membership ($14/month). They have live support chat for Plus Membership cus-tomers and a forum that answers many setup and maintenance questions. I do recommend using the Plus Membership at least until you completely set up your WordPress website—you'll be able to get life support from PageLines staff during each step.

Don't use themes created by unknown programmers or Word-Press developers. Avoid the use of any sponsored themes that contain the so called sponsored links. Any link to an outside source devaluates your site and is bad SEO practice. If you want a free theme, download one only from http://wordpress.org/extend/themes/ or a reputable theme developer like http://www.pagelines.com/ or http://www.studiopress.com/.

2. Adjust Privacy Settings

WordPress has privacy settings. If you want your WordPress website to be visible to search engines, you should check the option *Allow Search Engines to Index the site* in your privacy settings in the admin menu of your WordPress. Go to Settings, then Privacy, and check the option.

3. Set Up H1, H2, and H3 Tags

You should set up your WordPress to have the titles of individual posts to be in H1 tags. The same titles must be in H2 tags on the posts page of your blog (the page with all the posts, which must be excerpts; see *5 Make Posts on Posts Page Excerpts* below). Because I use the PageLines theme, I have this set by default, but if your theme was created by a developer, you should ask them to do this for you. It requires very small changes to the code. Also any widgets or links that are someway important must have H3 tags and the rest must have no tags at all. These are fundamental SEO settings. Every Web page needs to have only one H1 tag, the most important of the three. You don't want your posts page to have multiple H1 tags—that's why the title of the excerpt must appear in H2, the second in importance. It is OK for your posts page to miss an H1 tag.

4. Choose a Preferred Domain (www or non-www)

You should set which of these two versions of your WordPress site you want Google and other search engines to index: *http:// www.yoursite.com* or *http://yoursite.com*. Both are correct as long as you are consistent with your choice. The version you choose is called preferred domain and is recommended by Google Webmaster Tools (http://support.google.com/webmasters/bin/answer.py?hl=en&answer=44231). Being recommended by Google is a reason enough to do it. You can find WordPress Address Settings in the Admin area (Settings, General, WordPress Address).

5. Set the Number of Posts Shown on Posts Page

You can do this by going to Reading Settings, under Settings in your admin menu. Generally, the less posts you have on your posts page, the faster your site will load. Each of the posts on your posts page must be an excerpt (See *5 Make Posts on Posts Page Excerpts* below). But at the same time, the posts page's purpose is to showcase your blog—the more excerpts of posts you show, the better for your users. The best number of posts shown on the posts page depends on how much space your individual post excerpts take. In my case, because I prefer excerpts with large images and full width text on my posts page (it's pretty to look at) I can allow no more than 10 posts. See the home page of `http://blog.leatherup.com` for an example of posts page with 10 post excerpts.

6. Make Posts on the Posts Page Excerpts

Excerpts reduce the length of posts on your posts page, allowing room for showcasing other posts and reducing the time it takes for your site to load. Another benefit of this is to avoid your site from being penalized by search engines for having duplicate content. By having the full post on your post page and on the separate URL of the post, you allow duplicate content. Though some people believe that excerpts on posts pages damage the user experience by creating an extra click to go to a full post, most I think will agree that the benefits of excerpts outweigh the advantages. I prefer excerpts that show at least 2-3 lines of text (about 30 words).

There are three main kinds of post excepts on posts page depending on whether you use thumbnail version of images or the normal size of images (the same size they appear in posts), or no images. I like my excerpts to have images and I like an image to show in an excerpt the way it appears in my post (as wide as the paragraph); it looks neat and draws more attention to the post. My favorite theme framework PageLines allows me to easily set up excerpts and image thumbnails in different sizes. If your theme doesn't allow this, ask your developer to set this up for you. Or find a theme that offers these options. Or you can use **Auto Excerpt Everywhere plug-in** by Serena Villa. After you install the plug-in, you'll find it in the Settings tab of your admin area. Set up the number of characters you want to show on each excerpt and the size of the thumbnail. I found that the image thumbnail option in this plug-in may not work with all themes, but even without an image, you'll be better off using the plug-in if you have no other option for creating excerpts on your posts page.

7. Install All-in-One SEO Pack Plug-In

This plug-in ads essential SEO features to WordPress, and its features must be used on every post. At this point, a one-time set-up should be performed:

1. **Enable the Plug-in:** Find All-in-One plug-in in the control-panel of WordPress—Settings, All in One SEO. Enable the plug-in by checking Enabled.

2. **Home Title:** The Home Title (the title of your home page) is useful to both search engines and users and will show in some search engine results, especially when people search for a blog on a specific topic. With time, when your WordPress blog or site becomes established and offers a good deal of content, the title can be adjusted to reflect what the blog or website is really about and what type of content it offers. For now, write a short title that tells users what you think your site will be about.

3. **Home Description:** This goes one step further than the Home Title and should give a more detailed description of what your site is about. This description should be

adjusted as the content on your site evolves. Ideally, some of the main keywords used in the Home Title, Home Description, and (below) Home Keywords should match.

4. Home Keywords: Under Home Keywords, include keywords that are or will be subjects and topics of the blog or site in general. Ideally, the Home Keywords should be similar to the blog categories (See *1 Create Categories* in *1 Plan Your Content* in *Chapter 3 Content SEO*).

5. Canonical URL: Check Canonical URL's. The purpose of canonical URL is to tell Google which of these two versions of your site you want Google to show—*www. yoursite.com* or *yoursite.com*. All-in-One SEO Pack will automatically generate canonical URL's for every post according to your WordPress Address Settings.

6. Rewrite Titles: Check rewrite titles. By checking Rewrite Titles, All-in-One SEO will automatically use the meta title you chose for your post plus this: | *Your Blog Name.* For instructions on inserting meta data on separate posts or pages go to *11 Create Meta Data* in *2 Create Fully Optimized Posts and Pages* in *Chapter 3 Content SEO*.

Here's an example of a meta title done this way: *List of Best Biker Songs - Motorcycle Songs | Motorcycle Blog of Leatherup.com.*

7. Don't Check The Rest: The other settings of All-in-One must not be activated. For Noindex, it's best to use a more advanced tool like Ultimate Noindex Nofollow Tool II (see next step).

8. Set Up Noindex and Nofollow Values

Install the Noindex and Nofollow plug-in. You have to use noindex value to pages that can create duplicate content of your site. If unnecessary duplicate content is indexed by search engines, it will compete with your featured content on search results and on top of that you can be penalized for by search engines for having that duplicate content. I use **Ultimate Noindex Nofollow Tool II** by Kilian Evang. After you install the plug-in, go to Settings, click the Ultimate Noindex tab, and check all the noindex options. Don't check the nofollow options. Most SEO people agree that it is not a good idea to use nofollow value for links from your site to your site.

9. Remove All Unnecessary Outbound Links

Outbound links are links that point away from your WordPress site. Unnecessary outbound links are harmful to your site's search engine ranking. A newly-installed WordPress would have at least one such link at the footer of your site pointing to word-press.org. Other outbound links pointing to `http://wordpress.org` may appear by default on the sidebar of your site. If you care about your site's ranking, you must remove those Word-Press links—they only help Wordpress.org's popularity. Remember that every time you link to another site without using the nofollow value (rel="nofollow") in the link, you are voting for that site's popularity in search results and at the same time you are transferring part of your own popularity to that site. Too much of this "transferring" can lead to your site's going down in search results.

10. Set the Permalinks

Now its time to create a permalink (URL) structure for your WordPress site. These two structures have worked perfectly for me:

1. **Blog Post Permalinks:** A common permalink architecture for WordPress blog posts includes the article published date plus the post name [/%year%/%month%/%date%/%postname%/ or yoursite.com /2012/06/01/your-post-name]. There are many theories about which is the best permalink architecture, but in my opinion this one is the best for a WordPress blog or any blog because it includes the published date, which shows how relevant an article is. The date also insures that the permalink is unique. Notice that all spam sites, use only the name of the article without a date because the owners of these sites want the spammy articles to look relevant forever. Permalink structure or anything on a information site that hides the date of creation of Web pages is bad user experience for me—no date and I don't want to read any longer. Spam! User experience is becoming the most important aspect of all Web applications.

To change the default WordPress permalink structure, from the admin area of your WordPress, go to Settings, Permalink Settings, and choose Day and Name.

2. **Page Permalinks:** WordPress by default creates permalinks without the date on WordPress pages (http://blog.leatherup.com/harley-davidson-motorcycles/). You don't have to set anything in your WordPress for this.

11. *Optimize Your WordPress Pinging*

Ping, in blogging, is a software that blogs use to notify ping servers that new content has been published. Ping servers on the other hand feed information to news aggretators like Google News and to blog search engines. Because by default WordPress is set up to ping every time you edit a post, this can create a problem with ping servers—your blog can get penalized or banned because you ping them too much or unnecessarily. That's why a good ping optimizer can be very helpful. I recommend **Cbnet Ping Optimizer plug-in.** Download it, install it, and include a complete list of ping servers. Here's a site that offers a complete list: `http://wptidbits.com/webs/250-complete-list-of-pingupdate-services/`

12. Set Up Google Analytics

Google Analytics is the most widely used and best website statistics service. Using Google Analytics for tracking the performance of a WordPress site is absolutely necessary—it's the most important tool in internet marketing. For easy setup of this service, install **Google Analytics for WordPress plug-in** by Joost de Valk.

> **1. Create a New Profile in Google Analytics**: After you install the plug-in, go to your Google Analytics account (create one if you don't have it). In your Google Analytics, click Admin and then click New Account.

> **2. Authenticate Your Site with Google Using the Plug-in:** Now go to Google Analytics Plug-in in your WordPress site (Settings, then Google Analytics) and click Authenticate with Google.

13. Create XML Sitemap

Sitemaps are important SEO tools—they assist search engines in locating your Web pages. A good XML sitemap plug-in for WordPress is **Google XML Sitemaps by Arne Brachhold.** Here's how you can set it up:

> **1. Install Google XML Sitemap plug-in**: Go to Settings and find XLM-Sitemap tab (this is the name it uses on the menu). Leave all default checked items and click Build Sitemap.

2. Submit XML Sitemap to Google: It is even better if you submit your new sitemap to Google in your Google Webmaster Tool account. If you don't have an account sign up for one, add your WordPress site and verify it. Google will ask you to verify your site—you can do this with your Google Analytics account (See above step—*11 Set Up Google Analytics*). After verifying, you can submit your sitemap by going to your Google Webmaster account, then Site Configuration (left side menu) and choose Sitemaps. Now click Add/Submit Sitemap—red button on your upper right hand side. You should fill in the blank with *sitemap.xml*.

14. *Create XML Sitemap for Videos*

An XML sitemap for videos tells Google where to search for your embedded content—most videos in blogs are embedded. The plug-in I use to create a sitemap for videos is **Google XML Sitemap for Videos by Amit Agarwal**. This plug-in creates a sitemap for the YouTube videos you embedded in your site. I wish, however, that there was a plug-in that created an XML sitemap that includes all the videos, not just those from You-Tube. I often embed videos from Vimeo.com and on my motorcycle blog I sometimes feature videos from Jay Leno's Garage website. To create a video sitemap with this plug-in:

1. Install the Plug-in: Now go to the Tools menu in your admin area and click Video Sitemap.

2. Generate Sitemap: You can do this by clicking on the button Generate Sitemap. Click on the sitemap file to check for error messages.

3. Submit Video Sitemap to Google: You will do this using your account at Google Webmaster Tools. Sign in your Google Webmaster Tools account, and select the website for which you want to submit your map. Under Site Configuration in the left hand side menu, click Sitemaps. Click Add/Test Sitemap red button and include the sitemap extension */sitemap-video.xml* and submit.

15. Create XML Sitemap for Images

It's a good idea to help search engines find more files on your website. You can help them by installing an XML sitemap for images. The plug-in I use for this job is called **Google XML Sitemap for Images by Amit Agarwal**. For installing, generating, and submitting your WordPress image sitemap, the steps are the same as for creating XML sitemap for videos (See *13 Create XML Sitemap for Videos* above.) The sitemap extension for images is */sitemap-image.xml*.

16. Create HTML Sitemap

An HTML sitemap can help search engines crawl your website better and it can also help users navigate it. An HTML sitemap will contain links to all your blog posts and pages. I use **Simple Sitemap plug-in by David Gwyer**.

1. **Install the Simple Sitemap Plug-In:** After you install the plug-in, the sitemap generates automatically. Now publish a new page (not post) called Sitemap and place this code in it: [simple-sitemap]

2. **Exclude Page with Sitemap from Navigation:** You will need to exclude the HTML sitemap from your Navigation because this page is not so important. To do this, you can use **Exclude Pages plug-in by Simon Wheatley.** Remember that after installing, you won't see Exclude Pages plug-in in the Settings—it will give you an option to exclude a page or post from the menu while you are editing it. Some themes may have the option for ex-

cluding pages from the menu (even WordPress may soon offer this feature by default). If your theme has that option you should use it instead of installing a plug-in.

17.   Link to Related Posts

One of your main concerns if your WordPress website is a blog is to keep your readers on it for as long as you can. The longer your readers stay on your blog, the better. In SEO terms this means low bounce rate and higher ranking in search results; in business terms, greater opportunity to monetize. One way to make your blog visitors stay longer is by linking related posts. You can do this by creating links manually on posts to previous posts. But in addition to this, you can use a plug-in that creates links at the end of your posts to previous posts. I've used both **Contextual Related Posts plug-in by Ajay D'Souza** and **Yet Another Related Posts plug-in by Michael Yoshitaka Erlewine**. Contextual Related Posts plug-in is simpler—it merely requires installation and all default settings are fine. You can change the number of posts you want to display if five seems too many. To see an example go to any blog post of *blog.leatherup.com*. Look for the five links under every post.

18.   Use Lazy Loading for Images

A lazy loading software can delay the start of a program until it is needed. A lazy loading WordPress plug-in can greatly improve the experience on a site that uses images. Such plug-in makes a WordPress post with images faster by loading only the images visible on the screen and eliminating the time for waiting a page to load. This improves user experience and has SEO benefits. For my blogs, I use **Lazy Load Plug-in by Dave Artz.** All you have to do is to install the plug-in and activate it—no further setting is required. It's easy to check if it works. After installing, go to one of your WordPress posts and see if they load faster and if images are loading as you look at them.

19. *Use Google Libraries*

Another way to speed your WordPress site is to use Google Libraries for loading code on your site instead of using your own site's rearouses. A library, in computing, is a collection of software code and data designed to help other programs to work faster and better. A widely recommended plug-in that uses Google Libraries is **Use Google Libraries plug-in by Jason Penney.** This plug-in allows your site to serve WordPress javascript libraries using Google's AJAX Library API. The plug-in requires just an installation and activation—no further setting is required.

20. *Use Social Bookmarking/Social Sharing Buttons*

Typically placed before or under every blog post, social bookmarking/social sharing buttons can help your site visitors quickly and easily share your content on social sites. This, in turn, will bring more visitors from social sites to your WordPress site. My favorite social sharing button plug-in is **AddThis by AddThis**. The plug-in allows you to place elegant buttons for the most important social sites (Facebook, Twitter, Google+). It also allows sharing via major email client services, bookmark services, and hundreds of other social media sites. AddThis offers you free analytics reports to help you understand your site's social traffic—the reports are alright, but I prefer Google Analytics Real-Time to measure the immediate impact of social media when I share something. Here's how to set up AddThis plug-in:

1. **Install and Set Up AddThis Plug-in:** After installing, find AddThis in the Settings tab and choose how you'd like your sharing buttons to display above and below your WordPress posts and pages.

2. Register for an AddThis Account to Get Analytics Reports: After you register, get your profile ID, you'll be able to link your AddThis plug-in with your AddThis.com account. To see the analytics reports, you must go to your AddThis.com account.

PS: My theme, PageLines, has a similar social sharing feature, but I prefer to use the AddThis plug-in because it looks better, offers way more opportunities to share, and is being updated constantly. The only drawback of AddThis plug-in is that it creates a weird extension at the end of all links (for example: `http://blog.leatherup.com/sturgis-motorcycle-rally/#.UHRsBRVX1M4`). The extension allows AddThis to track shares and create reports. Since I no longer use AddThis reports, I turned off the tracking to remove the ugly extensions on my links. You can do this too—go to AddThis plug-in tab, click Advanced and uncheck all options under *Have AddThis track* ...

21.   *Add Links to Your Social Media Accounts*

Most websites and blogs today feature links in the form of buttons to social media accounts. Many sites have these buttons at the header. If you use social media in your business or blogging, it's not a bad idea to place such buttons in your WordPress site. This way you'll direct new visitors to your social accounts where they can meet with other fans of your site, check out comments others made about you and participate in discussions.

If you decide to place social media links, make sure to give them nofollow value. The reason I use the rel="nofollow" in the links to my social media accounts is that I don't want to pass PageRank (`http://en.wikipedia.org/wiki/PageRank`) to social media sites. For those who don't know, giving a follow link takes away from your own website's PageRank and passes it to the site your are linking to.

In my motorcycle blog (http://blog.leatherup.com/) I use Page-Lines theme framework that allows me to easily place social media links to the header of my WordPress site. But the creators of PageLines, at least at the time I'm writing this, made those links follow links, so I had to change the file of the theme to make the links nofollow; to do that, I installed the Base Theme of Page-Lines—a basic WordPress child theme of PageLines Framework designed to help you customize your theme without modifying the core files of the framework. Here's an article on how to install the Base Theme of PageLines: http://www.pagelines.com/wiki/How_to_Use_the_Base_Theme

After installing the Base Theme, I asked a PageLines rep where to find the file with the social media links—you know now that I had to change the links to nofollow links. The file (*sections.php*) was in a folder of the framework called "branding" which was in another folder called "sections." From the framework theme files in the hosting account, I downloaded the whole folder (sections) containing the subfolder (branding) in which the file (*sections.php*) was. Then I opened the file (*sections.php*) with Windows Notepad and added a nofollow tag in each social media link (*<a target="_blank"* **rel="nofollow"** *href="%s" class="facebooklink"><img src="%s" alt="Facebook"/></a>*). Then I had to upload the main folder (sections) with the changed file to the main folder of the Base Theme of PageLines, and it worked. Yes, sounds a bit complicated, but mention these instructions to a PageLines rep or a more experienced WordPress developer and you'll complete this in 10 minutes.

22. *Give Visitors More Options to Leave Comments*

Here's a cliché: Comments are the lifeblood of blogs. The expression is hackneyed, but the idea expressed by it is true. Comments give blogs a social aspect, engaging site visitors, transforming blog posts into discussions. One of my favorite plug-ins is **Facebook Comments for WordPress by we8u**. This plug-in allows people to comment using their Facebook profile. I like this plug-in because after using it for a while I discovered that people feel more inclined to comment on blogs while signed in their Facebook profile. Check this popular articles on my motorcycle blog to see that a smaller number of people used the blog comments function compared to those who used the Facebook Comments plug-in function: http://blog.leatherup. com/2011/11/25/shelved-harley-davidson-trike-prototypes/

The Facebook Comments plug-in has many options for customizing to fit your WordPress theme. After you install and activate it, go to the plug-in page in your WordPress Settings menu to set it up. Facebook Comments plug-in requires you to create a new Facebook application (sounds technical but it's easy) and input the secret key and app ID into the plug-in's control panel.

23. Allow Visitors to Subscribe to Comments

Another way to add value for your WordPress visitors is to allow them to subscribe to comments and follow discussions on posts. Try **Subscribe to Comments Reloaded plug-in by camu**. The plug-in allows both those who leave a comment and those who don't to subscribe to a discussion.

Install and activate the plug-in—I didn't have to touch any of the default settings when I installed this on my blogs. Test the plug-in: subscribe to the comments of a post with and without leaving a comment. See how the plug-in works: Visit this article http://blog.leatherup.com/2011/03/22/the-15-best-motorcy- cling-roads-in-america-selected-by-ama/ and look near the bottom of the page for the following text: *Notify me of followup comments via e-mail. You can also subscribe without commenting.*

24. *Enable Web Caching*

Web caching can greatly improve the performance of your WordPress website. Among the many benefits of Web caching are reduced load time, improved user experience, and lower bandwidth costs. I had never seen such a visibly dramatic improvement in the overall speed and load time of a WordPress site until my first installation of a Web caching plug-in. Two WordPress plug-ins for Web Caching have high user ratings: **W3 Total Cache by Frederick Townes** (W3 EDGE) and WP Super Cache by donncha and automattic. I prefer W3 Total Cache—it worked smoothly with all my other plug-ins and it has a higher user rating than WP Super Cache. Here's how to set up W3 Total Cache plug-in:

> 1. **Install the Plug-In:** After installing, go to the control panel—you'll see a new submenu called Performance. For some reason, the author named the menu of the plug-in Performance instead of W3 Total Cache.
>
> 2. **Set It Up:** Setting up usually requires only installation—the default settings are fine. This is what I do to set this up: 1) I click on the General Settings. 2) I make sure the following are enabled: Database Cache, Object Cache, Browser Cache. 3) I make sure the following are unchecked: General, Minify, CDN, Varnish, Network Performance & Security powered by CloudFlare (See *3 Use CloudFlare* in *Chapter 2 Security Settings*). 4) I leave the default settings under Miscellaneous and Debug.

Warning: I tried the minify option in this plug-in but it messed up one of my sites—minify doesn't work for all sites anyway. If you decide to use the minify option, check your site to see if it runs properly. If not, the most probable cause is that you've checked the Minify option.

Also make sure that you don't have other Web cache plug-ins running on your WordPress. The author of the plug-in warns that there could be a conflict. To make sure, just go through your installed plug-ins.

25. Create a Favicon

A favicon (favorite icon) is the small image that represents a website on a Web browsers. Having a favicon can make your WordPress site stand out from others that don't have one. It can help you brand your site and increase its visibility in your visitors' favorites menu. PageLines, my WordPress theme framework has a favicon option. But if you are using a different theme that doesn't come with a favicon or doesn't allow you to upload one, you can use **Cbnet Favicon plug-in by chipbennett.**

After you install the plug-in, go to Settings in the admin menu and click on Cbnet Favicon. Now you can choose one of the favicons available from the plug-in, or better, you can create a customized image with your logo. The dimensions of a favicon are 16 x 16 pixels. If you don't have a logo, you can use the initials of your website's name to create one with a Photoshop.

26. Disable Hotlinking

Hotlinking, also called inline linking or leeching, is the practice of displaying an image stored on another website. If other websites display hotlinked images from your site, you are using and paying for extra bandwidth and your site may start running slow. To prevent this, you can disable hotlinking using your WordPress .htaccess file. If you are an experienced developer, you can go to the root directory of your WordPress and edit the .htaccess file by adding extra code. I'm not a programmer and I prefer to use a plug-in. I found a plug-in specifically developed for that purpose (Hotlink Protection plug-in by christopher-ross). But I found that Christopher's plug-in doesn't work with subdomains—my motorcycle blog is on a subdomain (http:// blog.leatherup.com/). An easy way to disable hotlinking even on a subdomain is to use **WP htaccess Control plug-in by antonioandra.de.** Here's how:

1. **Install the Plug-in:** After you install and activate it, go to Settings into the control panel and look for and click on *htaccess Control* tab to go to the control panel of the plug-in.

2. **Disable Hotlinking:** From the control panel of the plug-in, click on *htaccess Suggestions* tab. A menu of options will open. Look for *Disable image hotlinking.* In the space provided, you can place the link to an image to which you want all hotlinked images to be redirected, or if you don't want anything to show you can place an underscore sign (_). In my motorcycle blog, I redirect hotlinked images to an image that I created with Photoshop and uploaded to our main website leatherup.com. The image says *Hot Linking Disabled.* To see the image, go here: *http://images. leatherup.com/images/newsletter/image-hotlinking-disabled.jpg*

27. *Stick to the 100-Links-Per-Page Rule*

The 100-Links-Per-Page rule comes from Google Webmaster Guidelines saying that webmasters must keep it under 100 links per page. The idea is that a Web page with more than 100 links wouldn't, in general, be user-friendly. And it is possible that Google might consider your site spammy if many pages contain more than 100 links. Fixing this in WordPress is easy—decide which links on the sidebar are more important: your categories, latest posts, tags etc, and put the unimportant ones in drop-down menus. If you check http://blog.leatherup.com you'll see that I have about 70 links on my homepage and about 50 on each post.

Of course this is just a general rule and it's OK to have pages with more than 100 links, even 300, as long as it makes sense for the user (Last time I checked Wikipedia homepage had about 270 links). I'm planning to have links to all articles related to Sturgis on my Sturgis Motorcycle Rally page (`http://blog.leatherup.com/sturgis-motorcycle-rally/`). But I'll try to keep most other pages under 100 links.

28. *More Performance*

What else can you do to increase your WordPress site's performance—speed, user experience, stability? A website is never finished and new techniques and software constantly evolve. I'm sure that I'll find and use other plug-ins or swap the ones I'm using with something new and better.

There are some great performance plug-ins that I used before but are currently incompatible with my current configuration. One of these plug-ins is **WP Minify plug-in by Thaya Kareeson**, a plug-in that can help you speed up your WordPress site by reducing the loading time. In computing and programing languages, minification is the removing of unnecessary characters from a source code with the aim to make the code lighter and reduce the data that needs to be transferred. A lighter code increases speed and efficiency. WP Minify uses Google's Minify Engine to combine and compress JavaScript and CSS files, and it requires only an installation and activation to work. W3 Total Cache plug-in (See *24 Enable Web Caching* above) also has a minify option.

If you decide to try WP Minify plug-in, check your WordPress site after installing it to see if it loads properly on all major Web browsers, especially on Internet Explorer. In my motorcycle blog when I used an Artisteer-generated theme before I switched to PageLines, the WP Minify plug-in prevented the social sharing buttons of the AddThis plug-in from displaying on the posts page (See more about AddThis above—*20 Use Social Bookmarking/Social Sharing Buttons*). Minify also made the site look messed up on Internet Explorer and interfered with Google Custom Search plug-in (another great plug-in I no longer use—see why below) forcing the results of the search to appear only in the widget box. WP Minify plug-in currently doesn't work with my current theme on `http://blog.leatherup.com`.

Another great plug-in I'm not using in my configuration is **Google Custom Search plug-in by edwinkwan,** a plug-in that significantly improves site search. WordPress site search sorts results by date and doesn't always give you the most relevant results. That's why installing a search plug-in can greatly improve your site's user experience. Steve Krug, the author of *Don't Make Me Think*, the book regarded as an authority in Web design, stressed the importance of having relevant site search. According to Krug, "some people will almost always look for a search box as soon as they enter a site. (These may be the same people who look for the nearest clerk as soon as they enter a store.)"

Before I started using PageLines framework as my theme on my motorcycle blog, Google Custom Search plug-in worked well. The reason I'm not using it right now is because my PageLines theme makes it hard to implement. The plug-in uses the power of the Google search engine—it can serve your readers relevant results from your WordPress site or even several other sites. You can configure it to serve the results in a pop-up window, under the search box, or anywhere in the site. I prefer the pop-up window—it looks neat and it doesn't show Google ads in the box even in the free version of the plug-in. Here I'll give the instructions for setting it up:

1. **Create a Custom Search Engine:** After you install the Google Custom Search plug-in, go to the plug-in in

the Settings tab of your WordPress. Find and click on the link to Google Custom Search (http://google.com/cse/). Click on the button Create Custom Search and configure your custom search engine.

2. Get Search Engine Unique ID from Google: Click on Basics settings and find the unique ID of your new search engine.

3. Enter your Search Engine's Unique ID: Now you can enter the ID into the settings of the plug-in.

4. Add the Google Custom Search Widget: Go to Appearance, then Widgets tab in your WordPress admin and add the Google Custom Search Widget to your site. The widget looks best on the sidebar where you'd usually have your search box. The only drawback of this widget is that it needs more horizontal space—I had to add pixels to the sidebar of the blog to fit it and I still didn't like how it looked.

5. Add Google Custom Site Search to Your Google Analytics Account: Adding your Google Custom Site search to your Analytics account will help you find how much your users use your site search. You'll be able to track visits (number of visitors who searched) and total unique searches. You need to have your Google Custom Search created with the same email that you use to log in as admin of the Google Analytics profile of your WordPress site. Go to the control panel of your newly created custom search in Google, click Analytics, find the Analytics profile of your WordPress site, and add these query parameters: term, search, query. You can find the Analytics data for your custom search in the Content side menu of your Google Analytics control panel.

CHAPTER 2

SECURITY SETTINGS

1. Create a Strong Admin Name and Password

Hackers use password cracking software to try to break into WordPress sites. Here's a fact: a password cracking software can guess at a rate of 1 billion combinations a second, and a five character password which contains 10 billion combinations can be guessed in 5 seconds. But you can make cracking your password very hard if you use 10 or more characters. You can make it almost unbreakable if you include upper and lower-case letters, numbers, and special characters. Creating a strong, secure password is one of the first things I do when creating a new WordPress site. I also change the default admin name (called admin). Here's what I do:

1. **Generate a Strong Password:** I first generate a strong password, using the strong-password generator from my favorite password-management software LastPass (try it, it's a great tool). You can also use a free secure password generators available online.

2. Create Another User: Go to your WordPress control-panel, find Users menu, and create a new user. Create a strong user name for that user (for example, John67234@) and don't forget to make it an administrator, not a subscriber, editor or author.

3. Delete the Default Admin Username: Using the word Admin as a username makes your account vulnerable.

2. Add Extra Security to Your Password

You can add extra security to your WordPress password by installing a plug-in. In all my WordPress sites I use **Login Lock-Down plug-in by Michael VanDeMar.** This plug-in records the data for every failed log-in attempt and disables the log-in after certain number of attempts. It will protect your site from hackers using the so-called brute-force cracking (trying every possible combination of characters). The plug-in requires installation only. You can leave the default settings.

3. Use CloudFlare

CloudFlare is a content delivery network—a system of servers and software that promises to make your website faster and safer. I mentioned CloudFlare in the previous chapter—CloudFlare can be set up together with W3 Total Cache plug-in. I use CloudFlare on several WordPress sites I maintain, and while I wasn't able to see improvement in site speed, I discovered how effective their software is in detecting site intrusion and resolving the effects of it. One of my WordPress websites was hacked recently—a hacker managed to inject malware disguised as a plug-in. CloudFlare detected the malware and I received a message from a representative with details about the problem, including where the malware files were, and tips on removing it. The CloudFlare team temporarily removed my site from their proxy server until I deleted the bad files. Here's how you can activate CloudFlare on your WordPress site:

1. **Create a CloudFlare Account:** Go to cloudflare.com and do it.

2. **Add Your Website:** After logging in your account, click on Add This Website.

3. **Change the Nameservers**: At the end of the process of adding a new website to your CloudFlare account, you'll be asked to change your current nameservers to those of CloudFlare. You'll go to your Web hosting provider account to do this. In my Web hosting provider, Bluehost.com, I can change the nameservers of my websites by going to Domain Manager, then Nameservers. When I click Nameservers, I can see an option for changing the Bluehost nameservers. If you need help, you can ask your hosting company—they know how it's done.

The only reason I'm not using CloudFlare on my motorcycle blog is that the blog is on a subdomain (http://blog.leatherup.com/) and I don't have control over the main domain (http://leatherup.com/). As long as you have control over the main Web address, you'll be able to set up CloudFlare using the instructions above.

4. Install Secure WordPress Plug-In

Secure WordPress plug-in by WebsiteDefender increases the security of your WordPress site by removing error information on login pages, adding *index.html* to plug-in directories, hiding the *wp-* version, and blocking bad queries that could be harmful to your website. Go to the plug-in page to see the full benefits of Secure WordPress plug-in—http://wordpress.org/extend/plugins/secure-wordpress/com/. To set it up:

1. Check All Boxes: After you install the plug-in, go to Settings, Secure WP, and check all the boxes that appear before Save Changes button. Click the Save Changes button.

2. Create a WebsiteDefender Account: Register at WebsiteDefender directly from the settings page of the plug-in. You won't be able to use the plug-in if you don't.

3. Log-in to WebsiteDefender: Now you'll have to log-in to your WebsiteDefender.com account.

4. Install a WebsiteDefender Agent: Website Defender will provide you with a small file (the agent) that you must install in the root directory of your WordPress site.

After you install the agent file, go back to your WebsiteDefender settings in your WordPress admin panel. The settings page will now show three boxes under Website Status on WebsiteDefender. The plug-in is completely set-up after all three boxes become green: Enabled, Scanned, Agent Status. Scanned will turn green after WebsiteDefender completes the scan, about an hour after you upload the agent file. The software will perform a scan once every week when you use the free version of their service (every day if you pay). You can manage all your WordPress sites with one WebsiteDefender account if you don't mind paying for their service. Otherwise you should open an account for every new site. You can log in to your WebsiteDefender account to check more advanced security features and status updates. For more information on how to set up WebsiteDefender go to http://www.websitedefender.com/getting-started/

5. Install WP Security Scan Plug-In

WP Security Scan plug-in by WebsiteDefender checks your WordPress site for vulnerabilities and suggests ways to solve them. Some of the suggestions it makes are more advanced and need backup before using—changing the *wp_ prefix* for example. The author of this plug-in is WebsiteDefender, so you'll use the same account you created for Secure WordPress plug-in (See *4 Install Secure WordPress Plug-In* above).

After installing the plug-in, you will have a small submenu of the plug-in in the admin area. Click on the first tab called WSD Security. This will show you how the plug-in fixed some security vulnerabilities (in green) and what should be done to protect your site further (in red). Installing could be the only action you perform with this plug-in if you decide that the other actions are too advanced for you. The creators of the plug-in say that it does what it is supposed to do as long as you keep it active. The other tabs from the WP Security Scan menu are less useful—you can generate a secure password for you admin account from other free software available online. For my WordPress sites, I just install the plug-in.

Warning: Changing the *wp_ prefix* in your database can protect you from SQL injection attacks. You can do this by going to Database tab of the plug-in. But you should backup your database before changing the prefix because it can disable some of your plug-ins.

6. Backup Your Site

Your WordPress site consists of two main parts: database and files. The database contains all your posts, pages, categories, and comments you've ever written. Your WordPress site consists of the following files: core installation; plug-ins; themes; images and files; javascripts, PHP scripts, and other code files; additional files and static Web pages. If your database gets corrupted, you can lose all the content you've created. If your WordPress files get erased or corrupted, you can lose all the work you've done on designing your site or setting it up to run properly.

I've tried several plug-ins that do automatic updates, but I found that they don't always work, especially if you have a large site with a lot of content. That's why the best way is to use your hosting company's FTP program. Find your site's WordPress files, and download them to your computer.

7. More Security

The list of things you must do to secure your WordPress site doesn't end here. You must, for example, regularly update your WordPress installation and plug-ins, use only plug-ins and themes created by reputable developers etc. But I decided to move these into *Chapter 4 Maintenance & Further Development*—it makes more sense since the first two chapters are meant to serve as a to-do list for setting up your WordPress site.

PART II

CONTENT & MAINTENANCE

In Part I, we went through the first steps in setting up a WordPress installation. Part II deals with creating and optimizing your content and maintaining your WordPress site.

CHAPTER 3

CONTENT SEO

1. Plan Your Content

Whether you plan a static site or a blog, planning your content in advance has many advantages. First, it will help you be more productive and organized in crafting your posts or pages. It will also help your readers in finding what they want, making them more likely to come back and stay longer on your site. This in turn, will signal search engines that your site is valued by visitors, which will result in higher placement in search results. Search engines also recognize and favor well-organized sites. Each subject in your new site can be made into a category where individual posts will be topics of that category. A larger and more important topic can be made into a category itself and divided into subtopics using separate posts.

1. **Create Categories:** Many professional bloggers believe that it's best to have as few categories as possible. This simplifies the task of a blogger and makes for more structured site. I believe that you should have as many

categories as you feel have to. For my motorcycle blog, I created about 50 categories—I like to categorize things because the world makes more sense to me when it's categorized. What I do, however, is to feature only the most popular categories in the main menu of the site; currently I feature two popular categories and the rest can be found under *Categories* button also in the main menu (http://blog.leatherup.com).

Before you create your categories, do some research in the field. Find websites that offer similar content—you can use these sites later as your sources for your own content. I'm always on the look for new interesting sources for my content, and every time I find a new source I bookmark it in my browser and add it in my Google Bookmarks—this Google service allows you to save your bookmarks permanently online. Look for blogs that offer news in your field, for brand sites that make products in your field, and remember to check the social media and social bookmarking sites related to such sources.

Use Google AdWords Keyword Tool (https://adwords. google.com/o/KeywordTool) to research the popularity of the phrases and keywords you plan to use in your categories. People may search for the same subject differently.

Blog categories are useful to the reader and to the search engines—think of them as online books made of articles on the same subject. Categories should be part of the overall blog navigation. Make sure that each post on your blog fits and is placed in at least one category and that each category has more than one post.

2. Create Tags After Creating a Post: WordPress tags are similar to categories. Tags, however, allow you to describe your blog posts in more specific terms, without having to add more categories. For example, if you are writing an article that goes to your chess strategy category and you mention how Garry Kasparov used this same strategy in a game, you can create a *Garry Kasparov* tag or a tag mentioning the game in which he used that strategy; say *Kasparov-Karpov, Game 48, World Campionship, 1985*. You should create tags on the fly, after you've written a blog post, and never create tags that are identical to blog categories.

I stopped using blog tags a while ago because I though they cluttered the space under my posts and reduce the importance of my categories. But I'm considering using tags again, this time moderately.

2. Create Fully Optimized Posts and Pages

A good practice for crafting your WordPress posts and pages is to create a posting routine. My posting routine usually follows this order: research topics, research keywords, open WordPress admin panel and click Add New (post), write the post title, write the post, find images, optimize images, place images in post (same applies to videos if I want a video in the post), write meta title for the post, write meta description, rewrite the permalink (WordPress creates an permalink identical to your article title and it's best to change it), place article in correct categories and/or tags, choose a featured image, preview article before posting, post the article, clear site cache (W3 Total Cache plug-in needs this to be done manually), and finally share the article on social media sites. It's a posting routine I refined through the years. Here's a checklist for you to follow when crafting a WordPress post or page.

1. **Research Your Topic:** The process of creating an article usually starts with some research—reading other blogs that offer content similar to yours for example.

Other times a blog post can be created from scratch. Even if you are creating a blog post from scratch, it always turns out better if written after researching into how other bloggers have written a similar blog post.

2. Research Your Keywords: Research related keywords and keyword phrases for your article before you write it; try to find the keywords people use when searching for the subject or topic you're writing about. Don't rely on what you read or see in other blogs—most bloggers don't do keyword research before posting, and if you do, your posts will be one step ahead in this aspect. The most popular and easy to use keyword research tool is the Google AdWords Keyword Tool (`https://adwords.google.com/o/ KeywordTool`). Use the keywords and keyword phrases you researched in the body of the article, in the article title (H1), subtitles (H2), *image title*, *image alt text*, *meta title*, *meta keywords*, and *meta description*, and mention the main keywords as early as possible in the first sentence of your first paragraph. You can also place the first mention of your main keywords in boldface, but don't do that every single time and don't use exactly the same long string of keyword phrases in all meta data—there's such thing called over-optimization for which Google may punish your site.

3. Optimize Post Length: More is bore. A general rule about length of blog posts is that the body text shouldn't be longer than 250-300 words. It's OK to have a blog post whose only content is one photo and one-sentence comment. But a post with ten long paragraphs is too long. If your post becomes too long, consider dividing it into two or three separate posts. If the content is closely related, you can divide the post into parts—say, *Sturgis 2012— Photos from the Buffalo Chip Campground, Part II.*

4. **Mix Your Content** (text, images, video): Whenever you can, try to mix the type of content within posts. Posts with photos or embedded videos in them are more interesting. Plus, Google has image and video search that can give your media-rich posts more opportunity for exposure in search results.

5. **Embed videos from YouTube:** Here I'm talking about using YouTube to get other people's content and create your own out of it. YouTube ads 48 hours of videos on any subject every minute, and most of those videos are free to embed on blogs. Embedded videos from others can be a great source of free and easy-to-post content—sometimes all you need for an interesting post is a clever comment with an embedded video. But when one video is your main content in a blog post, find an image that you can feature just before the video, as in this article (http://blog.leatherup.com/2012/08/01/official-2012-sturgis-promotional-music-video/). Having at least one image in the post allows you to set up a featured image for the post, and this featured image goes with the feed of the post. If you don't have a featured image, people will be less likely to click on a link to a post when, for example, that link is shared on Facebook or other social sites. (See 6. *Optimize Your Images* below; see more about featured images in WordPress: http://en.support.wordpress.com/featured-images/).

6. **Optimize Your Images:** Images are important—they attract attention. They are important for content that would be shared on social sites like Facebook, Google +, and Twitter; when you share a link to an article on your Facebook wall, a thumbnail version of one of the images in the article appears next to the title and description of the article and people are more likely to click on a link if the link contains a thumbnail photo.

I think that every serious blogger should learn how to use Photoshop for optimizing images for the Web. It's not hard at all. Images that are too big, slow down the loading of pages and posts. To optimize an image for the Web using Photoshop, open an image with the program, reduce its size to fit the width of your paragraphs (Image, Image Size, OK), and save for Web and devices (Ctrl + Alt + Shift + S).

The best way to include images in a blog post is to make them exactly as wide as a paragraph. You can start a post with a photo, then you can include text and another photo under it. Also include an *image title* and an *image alt text* (WordPress makes that easy to do). Image titles are less important but provide additional information to users and search engines. Alt texts provides information to users who cannot see the image (if users have their images disabled on their browsers for instance). In addition, Google focuses on alt text when trying to understand what an image is about (I, for example, use the same text for the image title and alt text —I don't think that the extra effort for creating separate text for both on any image is worth it). When adding an image title and an alt text to an image, try to use some of the keywords that you researched for the article but make the title and alt different. If you are willing to put an extra effort, keep the image title short and make the alt text more descriptive.

7. Optimize the Title (Heading) of Your Article: The heading of your WordPress post or article is the title that your readers see. Here you can go two ways—you can write a descriptive line of what is to follow in the body text, or you can write something catchy.

For many of my posts, I prefer a catchy headline; these posts usually contain some curious fact that I discovered for my regular readers and that often becomes popular on social media sites (goes viral as they say). See this viral post of mine with the catchy title *Video: Harley-Davidson Rat Bike Chopper Smokes Honda CBR1000RR Fireblade – 3 Times:* http://blog.leatherup.com/2012/06/01/harley-vs-honda-harley-davidson-rat-bike-chopper-smokes-honda-cbr1000rr-fireblade-in-drag-race/. If you want to hone your catchy-headline crafting skills, check this article: http://goinswriter.com/catchy-headlines/

Not all article headlines need to be catchy. Sometimes a descriptive phrase works just fine, normally when you report a piece of news: http://blog.leatherup.com/2011/11/25/shelved-harley-davidson-trike-proto-types/

Whatever headline you craft, it's always good to include in it the main keywords you researched before you wrote your article—keywords that appear in the headline are given more weight by search engines.

8. Optimize the Permalink of Your Article: You should create a custom permalink for your WordPress article. The permalink gives you an opportunity to include important keywords that are not in the heading. For example, I titled an article *Tsunami Motorcycle Goes to a Harley-Davidson Museum* but I created a custom permalink that includes the word *Japanese* in front of the word *tsunami.* Here's the permalink for this article: (http://blog.leatherup.com/2012/05/25/japanese-tsunami-motorcy-cle-goes-to-a-harley-davidson-museum/).

9. Use the Correct H Tag in the Subtitles: If your paragraphs need subtitles, make them H2 or H3 headings but never H1 because text in H1 tags is reserved for the title of a post—the title of the post that your blog readers see (also called heading), not the meta title. Here's an example article in which I used H2 titles. The main title of the article is *2013 Harley-Davidson Lineup – Overview (Part 1)* (`http://blog.leatherup.com/2012/08/23/2013-harley-davidson-motorcycles-lineup-overview-part-1/`). Notice that each subtitle in H2 could be a stand-alone blog post, though I decided to place everything in one post.

I don't use subtitles for my blog posts very often. The reason is that each time I though I needed subtitles it turned out that I could split the post instead and use the subtitles as topics for other posts.

10. Place Your Post in the Correct Blog Categories: I already discussed categories in the beginning of this chapter. Make sure you place your blog post or page in the correct category or categories.

11. Place Posts in the Correct Blog Tags: If you decided to use tags in your posts, now it's the time to create some that fit the post. If you found similar tags that you already used, don't create new tags. WordPress allows you to easily find tags that you already used on other posts.

12. Use Links Correctly: You should be very careful when creating links in your posts. A link can be created in a text or in an image. When creating an in-text link, remember to include an alt text.

If you are using your blog posts to build backlins to another site, don't create links on exact keywords because this makes it too obvious for your readers and search engines who might think that the sole purpose of your post is to build links. Instead, try to make links of longer phrases that include the keyword (*Check for Kawasaki parts in leatherup.com's motorcycle parts category*.). This practice was recommended by my coworker Tim, who's a link building specialist. Google favors links that look "more natural." And if your main purpose in writing a blog post is to build backlins to another site, try at least to limit the number of backlinks per post to a minimum because you will drain your posts and thus your entire blog from PageRank.

When you cite a source on your blog post, it is a good practice to provide a link to the source, but remember to add a nofollow meta data to the link so that you don't pass PageRank to the external page. Here's how the HTML code of a nofollow link looks like in an article of mine:

```
<a title=" Silodrome" href="http://blog.leatherup.
com/" rel="nofollow">Motorcycle Blog of Leatherup.
com</a>.
```

13. Include Meta Data: Every blog post, once created, becomes a separate Web page on your blog, and this page needs to be optimized for search engines using a meta title, meta keywords, and a meta description. The home page of the blog must have its own meta data (See *6 Install All-in-One SEO Pack Plug-In* in *Chapter 1 Performance Settings*), and every page its own unique meta data. If you haven't done this before, but you've been blogging for a while, this must be very easy for you to do using the options of All in One SEO Pack plug-in. The plug-in gives you options every time you are adding a new post or page. Look for All in One SEO Pack options at the bottom of the page when you are adding a new post.

Each set of meta data should use the main and secondary keywords you researched and chose for your article. The meta title of an individual post should be short and descriptive—you can paraphrase the heading of the post and use it as a meta title. A good way to create a meta description for a blog post is creating a short description of what the blog post is about. The All in One SEO Pack also offers you an option to repeat the keywords and add others: include only the main keywords divided by comma—don't stuff your posts with keywords because this is considered spam by search engines and they may lower the rank of your post for doing so.

14. Check the HTML Version of Your Article: Every WordPress post and page has an HTML version and every professional blogger needs to know the basics of this version—to recognize when the code is broken, to see if there's something missing, to optimize the links using the correct tags (See *Use Links Correctly* above) etc. It's not hard to learn the basics if you compare the correct older HTML version of a WordPress post with a new one. With time, after some practice, you'll need just one look to tell whether there's something wrong in the HTML code.

I write my WordPress posts in the HTML version because this gives me a complete control over the code. (See this article about writing posts from WordPress.org: `http:// codex.wordpress.org/Writing_Posts#Visual_Versus_ HTML_Editor`).

15. Clear Cache Every Time: If you are using **W3 Total Cache plug-in** like me, clear all caches every time you create or update a post or page. If you don't, site users may not be able to see your update. Just click once on Clear All Caches in the plug-in menu on top of your admin panel and you are done.

16. Share Your Content on Social Media Sites: The biggest thing that can happen to any blog is to get discovered by the right audience. This is why a good practice after the creation of every post is to share it on popular social bookmarking sites like StumbleUpon and Pinterest—and social networking sites like Facebook, Twitter, and Google+. Use the social sharing button on the post to share. (If you don't have social sharing button on your blog, go to *20 Use Social Bookmarking/Social Sharing Buttons* in *Chapter 1* for instructions on how to install a popular plug-in).

Both social bookmarking and social networking sites, or to be precise—their users, can greatly benefit your site. Users from those sites, provided that they like your content, will further share the page that you shared with them; they will make comments on the link you provided and you will receive Internet traffic, sometimes significant amounts of traffic back to your site depending on how much your story picks up. Some of those who read your post, may join your regular readers and your subscription list.

Search engines now give priority to content that is being shared and given attention to in social media; the reason is clear—if a Web page is shared and people leave comments on it or about it on other sites, it means that the users are interested in the content; and that's exactly what search engines are supposed to serve to other users.

Now let me share my experience about, ahem, sharing with individual social media sites. First, I don't share on all social media sites, which is not only physically impossible but impractical. I share only on the most important ones.

- **Share on Facebook:** If you have a business related to your WordPress site, it's best to open a Facebook Page and share your WordPress posts there. If your site is not related to a business, make a Facebook Page carrying the name of your WordPress site. For best results and if you have the funds, you should also use Facebook Advertising (Facebook Ads: `https://www.facebook.com/about/ads/`) to build audience for your Page faster. If you have a big circle of friends and acquaintances and if you don't mind, you should also share your posts in your personal Facebook account.

When you share on Facebook, when you provide the link to your new WordPress post, try to make some interesting comment about the link, something you think would make others interested and prompt them to click on the link or make a comment about what you said. See how I do it on the Facebook Page of Leatherup.com (`http://www.facebook.com/LeatherUp`).

Monitor your Facebook Page daily, answer people's questions, participate in conversations you started with your followers, and post an update no more than three times a day.

• **Share on Twitter:** Twitter status updates are similar to those on Facebook. But Twitter is considered real time and needs to be updated more often than Facebook; people don't read old tweets. And while Facebook is a good place to start a conversation with your fans or customers, Twitter isn't—its purpose is to offer quick updates and news. That's why on your Twitter account, it is OK to share links to content from other websites related to your industry in addition to sharing stuff from your blog. In the beginning of this chapter

(Planning Your Content), I mentioned that you should bookmark and keep track of websites or other blogs in your field and use them as sources for your own content. Another way to use these sites is to share their content on your Twitter account.

From the perspective of your Twitter account having the full benefit to your WordPress site, you should be updating your Twitter account often—three to four times every day if possible with quick news about your filed or industry. To build more audience for your Twitter profile, don't follow everyone—you are allowed only 2000 followers—but research how others are doing it and try Twitter Advertising: (https://business.twitter.com/).

• **Share on StumbleUpon:** StumbleUpon is my favorite social bookmarking site. When you share something really good on StumbleUpon, you will get tons of Internet traffic back to your WordPress site. A "Stumble" from the right user can create a snowball effect and you can end up with a lot of short term visits from the site. But the best thing is that good "Stumbles" (links) can keep bringing you traffic and new visitors for years. When you share a story from your WordPress blog on StumbleUpon, also take a few minutes to discover other sites discussing the same subjects as your blog. Or share some news story from these sources of yours I talk about all the time. If you don't share and rate stuff, and if you keep "Stumbling" only your own WordPress posts, your account will obviously look like a self-promotion; it won't persuade anyone to look at your content and you may even get banned from the StumbleUpon.

Another great advantage from using StumbleUpon is that you may find great new sources of content for your own blog.

Before or after I share an article of mine on StumbleUpon, I "Stumble" a few things from my field. To "Stumble" things in your other people's content in your field, type in StumbleUpon's search bar the keyword you are looking for.

Check out this forum post about people discussing StumbleUpon: http://www.webmasterworld. com/link_development/3629897.htm. Also check this article called "How to Make Your Blog Big on StumbleUpon": http://www.stumbleupon.com/ blog/how-to-make-your-blog-big-on-stumble- upon/.

• **Share on Pinterest:** Pinterest is a social photo sharing site, the fastest growing social site. And because a significantly larger percent of Pinterest users in the United States are women, the site gives bloggers an opportunity to tap into the female audience. There was a study earlier this year according to which Pinterest drove more traffic to retailers than YouTube, Google+ and LinkedIn combined together. And from my experience, Pinterest has a potential for driving good traffic to blogs. Currently the Motorcycle Blog of Leatherup.com receives more referrals from Pinterest than from Twitter. But you should know that to receive traffic from Pinterest, your blog needs to offer good, interesting images. For example, in the Leatherup Blog I often post images of custom bikes, biker women, new motorcycle products—

photos that speak for themselves. I avoid using stock photos.

Before you start sharing your images on Pinterest, or "Pin" them as they call it, take time to research the categories in which to "Pin" your images, the people or accounts with most followers in your field, and the most popular collections of pins in your field. To do that, type a keyword or phrase in the search bar; you will get three types of search results: pins, boards, and people. From the pins and boards you can get some good material to "RePin" and grow your own account, plus you may find things you want to post in your own blog.

• **Share on Google+:** My Google+ Pages send very few referrals to any of my blogs. Google+ Pages are similar in structure and function to Facebook Pages (Read about Facebook above). Right now, I'm using Google+ for one reason only, and that is: Google favors its own social network in search results.

• **Share on Other Social Sites:** If you have the time and resources, you can try sharing your blog content on other popular social sites like Digg, Reddit, or Delicious. It won't hurt. But remember that all you may need is to develop one or two social media accounts (say a Facebook Page representing your WordPress site or business and a Twitter Profile representing you as an author) and use them for what they are supposed to be used; otherwise to users you'll look like a spammer pushing his own agenda; you won't sound genuine and you may never be able to build an authority.

CHAPTER 4

MAINTENANCE &
FURTHER
DEVELOPMENT

1. *Update WordPress Installation, Plug-Ins, and Themes*

WordPress is an open source software and needs to be updated every time a new version comes. The same applies to WordPress plug-ins and themes. If you don't update, your site will become vulnerable to intrusion. Make updating your WordPress installation and plug-ins a habit. Every time you open the control panel look for available updates.

2. *Use Plug-Ins and Themes Created by Reputable Developers*

Use plug-ins and themes that are updated regularly and created by reputable developers. You won't have any problems if you use the plug-ins and themes I recommend in this book. But if you decide to use other plug-ins, research them before you install them to see user reviews and requirements and whether their authors have been updating them regularly.

3. Delete Unused Plug-ins

You must delete all unused plug-ins. Unused, disabled plug-ins can affect the load time of your WordPress site. Each time a visitor opens a page on your site, the database is checked to determine what should be loaded on the page an what not and the disabled plug-ins will be on the list. Having unused plug-ins also puts your site at risk of being hacked.

4. Optimize Your Database

Once in a while you'll need to clean up your WordPress database. **Install WP-Optimize plug-in**: This plug-in that does this job well. In a few clicks, it can remove all unnecessary information and files from your database including post revisions and drafts, spam comments, and unapproved comments. It also shows how much space you can save and how much information can be deleted.

Cleaning your database can improve the speed of your website. Every revision or update of a post, saves a copy of that post. If you edit your post 3 times, you'll end up with 3 instead of 1 copy of your post in your database. According to the this plug-in, the amount of post revisions I collected in http://blog.leatherup. com/ for the 2 and a half years before I installed WP-Optimize was 5077; the number of posts and the number of spam comments amounted to 20MB and I was able to save that space by deleting the unnecessary files with one click. In my personal blog kalinnacheff.com it showed that I had 221 revisions just after 5 posts! I revise a lot. After you install the plug-in, a link (WP-Optimize) will appear your admin area under Settings. Click on the link to set up the plug-in:

> 1. **Check all Options** that Need Optimization: Under Database Optimization Options in the plug-in menu, check the options that need optimization. The ones that

need optimization will have numbers under them (how many post revisions need to be deleted etc). If you look below, you'll see how much space can be saved by deleting the unnecessary files.

2. **Click Process Button:** This will clean up your database. The plug-in will show you a report saying how many of each has been deleted and how much space has been saved. For example: *221 post revisions deleted, 1 autodrafts deleted, 2 spam comments deleted.* You can go through the cleanup process every time you create a new post or on a schedule you feel comfortable with.

5. Discover Keywords To Develop Further

If you've had a blog for a while and if you've learned how to use Google Analytics, you probably know that a large portions of your search engine traffic comes from a few keyword phrases. This means that your WordPress site is already considered an authority for these phrases in search engines and you can keep building on this authority to boost traffic, provided that these keyword phrases and topics are something you want to rank for. If you want to get traffic from other keywords, you need to create content for them. To find your best performing keywords of all time using Google Analytics: choose the period (from...to...); go to Traffic Sources, Search, Organic; and you'll see a list of keywords arranged in order of importance.

Another way to keep track of the keyword phrases your website ranks for is to use **Rank Reporter plug-in**—I used it in my motorcycle blog.

Years ago, I discovered that my motorcycle blog received a considerable traffic from keywords related to the Sturgis Motorcycle Rally. I had several articles on the rally and because I was already an authority on other keywords and subjects related to motorcycling, Google decided to show articles about the rally on my blog high in the search results. Obviously, the Sturgis keywords and the topic of Sturgis had a big potential.

6. *Create More Content Using Keywords You Rank For*

The best way to increase traffic from search engines from keywords you already rank on search engines, is to create more content. Create content with similar or related topics using the keywords you discovered.

1. Post Articles on the Same Subject, Using the Same Or Similar Keywords: After I found that articles related to the Sturgis Motorcycle Rally perform well, I started creating more articles on the subject. Sturgis-related keywords are seasonal, meaning that most people search about the rally just before, during, and after the rally. That's why I create most of my Sturgis articles around this time—looking for news and interesting facts about the event.

2. Create Categories: When you have several articles that perform well on a certain keyword and if you don't have a category having that keyword, it's time to create one and put the articles in it. In the case with Sturgis, I created a category right after I wrote my very first article because I did some research and found that the rally was an important topic in the motorcycle community—it's the biggest in the world.

When you develop the subject further, you may find that creating subcategories might be a good idea. For example, in my motorcycle blog I've had a category called motorcycles for a while, until one day I decided to split it into subcategories for each major brand. This way readers who were interested in Harley-Davidson could directly go to that category for information and news. Avoid creating "empty" categories—search engines don't like that.

3. Create Category Pages on Your Main Menu: When you have a considerable amount of traffic coming from articles in a certain category, it's good idea to feature the category in your main navigation menu. I'm talking about not linking to the page where all the posts in a category show, but linking to a Web page you create that will show your posts from that category in a feed. By doing this, you will feature the well-performing content for your site visitors and you will also give a signal to search engines that this category (and its keywords) is important in your site. Search engines give prominence to things featured in your main menu and the page will soon get a higher PageRank than most others in your blog.

Also, you can start **linking future posts in that category to this category page** to build even more PageRank and search engine authority to it. Use a prominently placed follow in-text link when linking to that page. You can also find all older posts in this category to create more in-text links to that page.

Here's what I did for my motorcycle blog: I created a page called Sturgis Motorcycle Rally that contains a short text introducing the subject and a feed featuring all the articles in the category starting with the newest posts: (http://blog.leatherup.com/sturgis-motorcycle-rally/). To create the feed, I used **RSS in Page plug-in by Titus Bicknell.** After installing RSS in Page, I placed the short code in the HTML version of the page. The code in my motorcycle blog is [rssinpage rssfeed='http://blog.leath-erup.com/category/events/motorcycle-rallies/sturgis-motorcycle-rally/feed/' rssformat='Y' rssitems='15000'].

Because the default setting of WordPress allowed only the 10 most recent feeds to show, I had to use **RSS Manager plug-in by ajayver** to make all the articles in that category appear in the feed. But after a month, I disabled the RSS Manager plug-in and the RSS in Page plug-in worked without it, showing all the articles in the Sturgis category. I've set the RSS in Page plug-in to show 15000 articles so that I have every article in the Sturgis category shown on the page.

4. Create Sub-Category Pages: When you collect even larger amounts of content on a specific popular subject, you can start breaking it down into sub-categories; you can now create a sub-category page of the main category page on your main menu. Your main category page will become a drop-down menu (or the first item on a drop-down menu) and users will be able to access the sub-category page from there.

I, for example, am about to create a sub-category page of my Sturgis Motorcycle Rally page called Sturgis 2012. To do this, I should find all the articles related to the Sturgis rally 2012, place them in a blog category called Sturgis 2012, and show the feed in my newly created page for Sturgis 2012. And of course I'll again make use of the **RSS in Page plug-in by Titus Bicknell** (See *Create Category Pages on Your Main Menu* above).

7. Optimize and Update Your Best Performing Posts/Pages

Every website has one or several best performing pages or posts—the ones that bring the most amount of traffic from search engines. If it's not obvious which are your best performing posts or pages, you can find this out easily with Google Analytics—go to Google Analytics, Content, Overview and the software will show you your most visited pages for the last month (you can change the dates and see your most visited pages of all time, the past 6 moths, etc).

I found that Google recognizes even the slightest update on an older WordPress post or page; recently I set up featured images on several older posts and I saw an increase of traffic to them. The reason why Google likes to show results from older Web pages is that these pages already have authority. And when such pages are updated, there's even more chance of them to show up higher in search results.

8. Discover Content that Social Media Users Like

With time you'll discover that certain type of content performs well in social media after you share it. Sometimes a blog post may receive an enormous amount of comments and sometimes not that many comments but many, many views. When you discover something like that, you must make a habit of creating more similar content to share in social media.

APPENDIX A

MORE OFF-SITE SEO

1. *Submit Your WordPress Site to News Aggregators*

News aggregator websites, also called feed aggregators or feed readers, collect news for people looking for information about a particular subject. As opposed to search engines who index your site's Web pages, news aggretators index your RSS feed and can bring significant traffic to your WordPress blog. Popular news aggretators are Google News and AllTop.com, sites similar in the way ping servers work but for which you have to apply personally (See *11 Optimize Your WordPress Pingingin* in *Chapter 1 Performance Settings*). Google News and AllTop.com have many categories for almost all subjects. You can also try to find and submit your site to news aggretators in your niche — AffBuzz. com and AffDaily.com, for example, are affiliate marketing aggretators.

Read carefully the guidelines for submitting to AllTop.com (http://alltop.com/submission/) and Google News (http://

support.google.com/news/publisher/). I had to ask an AllTop rep to reconsider their initial decision to reject my submission of my motorcycle blog—and it worked. In my letter to the rep, I pointed out other sites already listed in the motorcycle category of AllTop that offer similar content. The Motorcycle Blog of Leatherup.com was initially at the bottom of AllTop's motorcycle category but now, a year later, it had climbed to the middle (http://motorcycles.alltop.com/).

Accepting your site into Google News is even harder (I'm still waiting for an answer after my second submission). First, your WordPress site needs to offer news stories almost every day. And second, you have to be able to meet Google News' technical requirements (http://support.google.com/news/publisher/). In the past, Google News required you a unique number in the URL. Today, with WordPress, this rule can be overridden if your site offers a Google News XML Sitemap. To create such a sitemap for your WordPress site, I recommend **Google News Sitemap plug-in by Andrea Pernici**.

Install the Google News Sitemap plug-in, and go to Settings, Google News Sitemap tab, and decide which categories and pages you want to exclude from the sitemap—you should trim out from the sitemap everything that isn't news. Then click rebuild. Remember that only posts created within the last 24 hours will be included in the sitemap, which is why you need to commit to report at least two pieces of news per day (otherwise your basket will be empty). Submit your Google News sitemap to Google in your Google Webmaster Tool account (See *Create Google XML Sitemap* in *Chapter 1 Performance* for information on how to submit a sitemap).

2. *Promote Your Site on User-Generated Content Sites*

A great way to promote your site is to create articles for sites such as HubPages.com, EzineArticles, Gather.com, and Squidoo.com. Do this the right way—create quality articles, give something to receiving something in return, and don't spam.

Years ago I maintained an e-cigarette blog, I haven't written anyting on it in a long time (www.e-cigarettepedia.com/) and I was also active on HubPages.com as an author (http://rainmakerrain.hubpages.com/). HubPages allows only original articles and splits the advertising revenue from articles 60/40 in favor of the authors. I decided to create an article about e-cigarettes and link it to my e-cigarette blog. The link became and remained the number one referral for the blog; I just checked it—it still is. Here's the article: (http://rainmakerrain.hubpages.com/hub/electronic_cigarettes_are_the_best_way_to_quit_smoking).

Why this single article has been having such a big impact on the blog? I had several successful articles on HubPages.com before, some of which were featured on the front page of HubPages and received a great number of comments. This made me an authority on the site; HubPages knew I wasn't a spammer, that my content was genuine and people liked it so they pushed my articles, making them more visible to site visitors. Naturally visitors clicked on the link I provided to my e-cigarette blog. Another benefit for the e-cigarette blog I didn't realize then was that the link was *follow,* which means that the e-cigarette blog received a vote from HubPages.com to be placed higher in search engine results. Hubpages has author score (HubRank) and the links created by authors who have a score above 75 (my score was above that) are follow links.

Enough for HubPages. My coworker, Tim, the SEO expert, has his own link building strategy involving user-generated sites. He told me that you can create an article, a good article with links to your target site, and then publish it to several user-generated content sites. Of course, you should know for what keywords you are building link authority and feature those words in your links. Here's a short description of his strategy:

1. **Choose the Keywords:** Decide for what keywords you want to build link authority.

2. **Write the Article:** An article that has one link to your target site for every 100 words.

3. **Submit the Article to User-Generated Content Sites:** EzineArticles.com, Gather.com, PubArticles.com, and SooperArticles.com. You should submit to Ezine first because they allow only original content, similar to HubPages.

3. Submit Press Releases

If you WordPress site or blog becomes very successful even when created to promote a given business, it can turn into a business in itself. After a content site becomes a business, you can apply to it other SEO techniques you would normally use to promote other types of websites or businesses. I'm talking about paid inclusion in search engine results or paid press release distribution. There are large, paid press release services like PRWeb. com and free or low cost press release services like Free-Press-Release.com.

An article distributed through large, paid press release service like PRWeb.com, EmailWire.com or PRLeap.com can bring tons of traffic to a site in a very short time. And if the story picks up, the article can help you create many links back to your site. It will also boost your site's PageRank—some press release articles can reach a PageRank of 5. A press release distributed through

PRWeb.com will cost you $200—make sure you really have something new to tell, otherwise your money can go to waste.

Free press release sites can also bring traffic and they can distribute your release to other sites as well. Some popular free press release sites are PRLog.com, openPR.com, and PressBox. com.

4. Even More Off-Site SEO

Of course there are many more ways to optimize your site.

1. **Leave Comments on Other Blogs:** Some bloggers leave comments on other blogs. Typically this involves creating a link back to your own blog. These links have no search engine value because most blogs automatically add nofollow tags to all comments. However, such links are good for branding your site and content and for reaching new audiences.

2. **Exchange Guest Posts with Other Bloggers:** Many bloggers do guest posts to exchange links. If you read what the gurus are saying out there, you would think that this is the best thing you can do to your blog, but I don't think it is. If you blog becomes successful like mine, you'll receive many inquiries. The reason I never allowed others to post in my motorcycle blog is that those who asked me were all kinds of "optimizers" and link builders for other people's sites, not a single genuine motorcycle enthusiast or a blogger. If I ever decide to hire a guest blogger for my motorcycle blog, I would make sure that he or she is a genuine author or expert in their niche.

3. **Submit Your Site to Online Directories:** Online directories organize websites into categories. They don't index pages like search engines do, just the website. Get-

ting your site into one of the two major directories is a very good thing. The Open Directory Project helps Google search results and the Yahoo! Directory helps Yahoo! Search.

Submit your blog to the Open Directory Project—it's free. Go to this page to read their instructions first (http://www.dmoz.org/docs/en/add.html). Now go to the main directory (http://www.dmoz.org) and through the categories—as deep as you can—to find the best ones to include your site in. When you are at a category, look for Suggest URL in the upper right corner of the page and click on it. Complete the form and you are done.

The Yahoo! Directory offers two kinds of submission—paid and free. If you want a guaranteed review of your site within 7 days it will cost you $299 recurring annual fee. I do recommend, provided that your WordPress site offers non-commercial content, to first try the free submission (http://add.yahoo.com/fast/add?2141115).

You can also try to list your WordPress site to some of the numerous specialized directories. A listing from such a directory can bring you small number of targeted visitors, plus it may have some search engine value if the link to your site has follow tags. To find specialized directories in your niche, try this free tool (http://www.soloseo. com/tools/linkSearch.html). Just type a keyword and go through the results for directories. Be careful, however. Most of these directories require you to provide a link back to them, which I don't recommend. With your link, you would probably give the directory more value than they would with theirs.

APPENDIX B

ADS

Many blogs are created and maintained for the purpose of promoting a business, just like my motorcycle blog (http://blog. leatherup.com/) promotes Leatherup.com. These blogs don't need to advertise anything except the business they represent but they still need strategically-placed banner ads.

Banner ads give direct exposure to your services and increase referral rates from your blog to your business pages. If you are an e-commerce business, your banner ads should lead to main sections of your products available to purchase online. I created the Appendix to show you how I managed to set up the banners in my blog, which will be invaluable to anyone maintaining a company blog.

1. Install AdRotate Plug-in by Arnan de Gans

This great plug-in offers a complete solution for offering ads on your WordPress site—you can create as many ads of different shapes and sizes as you want and place them anywhere you want. The plug-in also offers tracking reports—how many clicks per day etc. I use this plug-in to create and manage sidebar ads. For ads that appear in the content, I use AdRotate in combination with Simple Ads Manager plug-in because the latter allows me easier placement without the help of a programmer. After you install and activate the plug-in, you'll have a new tab added in your admin panel called AdRotate. Here's how I create and place my sidebar ads with AdRotate plug-in:

1. **Creating a Group:** First you can start by creating a group of ads—click on Manage Groups, Add New, and create a name for your group. Use a name that reflects where your group of ads will appear—for example, Sidebar Skyscraper Top (you may want another skyscraper banner in your sidebar at the bottom). In each group you can have as many ads as you create and they will rotate in the same place you place that group. Note that if you don't create at least one group where to place at least one ad, the plug-in will not work.

2. **Creating Ads:** To create an ad, go to Manage Ads and click Add New. Now give a name to your ad and choose an AdCode (for my ads on http://blog.leatherup.com/ I use this: **<a href="%link%"><img src="%image%" /></a>**). Don't forget to include the link that the add will lead to (Clicktracking) and check the box next to Clicktracking to allow the plug-in to track your ads. You also have to select a group for your ad. Everything else is pretty straightforward. You can create as many ads as you want and then you can place them in as many groups as

you want. For my motorcycle blog, I created two groups of ads for the right sidebar (the sidebar originally designed for placing ads).

3. **Placing Ads on the Sidebar:** To place ads on the sidebar, go to Appearance tab in the admin area and click on Widgets. Under Available Widgets, find the AdRotate widget and place it in the appropriate widget area, name the widget (the text will show above the ad) and choose between a group, ad, or block of ads to show. In my motorcycle blog I placed all the sidebar ads in the Secondary Sidebar (right sidebar) area, which starts from the top of the right sidebar of the blog. You can place as many AdRotate widgets in the sidebar as you want. I placed two AdRotate widgets in my motorcycle blog, one under the other—each of those widgets shows ads from one of the two groups of ads I created in advance. For each widget, I chose Group of Ads and put the ID name of each.

4. **Preparing Ads and Groups that Will Appear Before, in the Middle, or After Your Content:** You can now create these ads and place them in groups as in steps 1 and 2 above. For http://blog.leatherup.com/ I created one group of horizontal ads that appears just under the blog posts. To place this group of ads just under the posts, I used Simple Ads Manager plug-in (see below).

2. Install Simple Ads Manager Plug-In by Minimus

The AdRotate plug-in has a big drawback—it's not easy with it to place ads before, inside, and after the content of your WordPress site. That's why I use Ads Manager to help me place my AdRorate ads in or around the content of http://blog.leatherup.com/. Basically, I use the ad code (and the actual ads) generated with AdRotate to place inside the Simple Ads Plug-in—it's like placing ads within ads. The reason I don't use Simple Ads only is that AdRorate has an important feature for me—advanced click-tracking. If Simple Ads generated better click-tracking reports, I would probably quit using the AdRotate plug-in altogether. Installing the Simple Ads Manager Plug-in, will create a new add tab in your admin panel called Ads. To create your content ads—ads that can appear before, in the middle, or after your content:

1. **Create Ads Places:** Click on the Ads Places on the Simple Ads Menu and create a new Ad Place. This Ad Place will represent the group of horizontal ads you created with AdRorate (See step 4 in *1 Install AdRotate Plug-in by Arnan de Gans* above). Now name the ad place—use a name that will help you recognize it, a name that relates to where the ad is. I named an ad *Bottom Post Ad Horizontal* because it went just under my blog posts. Now select Custom Size and put the dimensions of the horizontal ads you created. Select HTML or Java Code, and use the following code as a model:

    ```
    <div style="margin-left:-10px;">

    [adrotate group="3"]

    </div>
    ```

    The first line helps you adjust your ad according to your blog posts (depending how many pixels you put (- or +). The second line of code is the group of horizontal ads you created with AdRorate (yours could be Group 2 for example). The third line is just a closing tag to make the code work.

2. **Set Up Your Ad in Settings:** To make the horizontal group of ads work, you'll need to go to the settings of Simple Ads Plug-in: Make sure your Ads Place (the one

you created in Simple Ads Plug-in) is selected under Ads Place After Content and that you check the two boxes: (1) Allow Ads Place auto inserting after post/page content and (2) Allow using predefined Ads Place HTML codes (before and after codes).